THIS BOOK BELONGS TO:

_____

THE WONDERFUL WORLD OF HIGHLAND COWS

MIMI JONES

Dedicated to all the Highland cow lovers out there.

ISBN 978-1-958985-63-2

www.joeysavestheday.com

A Mimi Book

Highland cows are known as "hairy coos" in Scotland because of their long, shaggy fur. "Coo" is the Scottish word for cow.

Highland cows have two layers of fur. The soft, fluffy layer underneath keeps them warm, and the long, oily hair on top helps keep them dry. In spring, they lose some of the fluffy fur, but their long hair keeps growing, so they stay warm all year.

Their fur can be red, black, white, yellow, or silver.

Highland cows have big, soulful eyes that make them look extra cute. Their long, wispy eyelashes aren't just for looks; they act as natural shields that keep out dust.

They are very hardy and can survive in tough weather conditions.

survive

Highland cows have big, curved horns that can grow up to 3 feet long! Both males and females have horns, and they use them to protect themselves.

Highland cows also use their strong horns to dig through snow when it's cold, helping them find grass and plants to eat.

Highland cows are herbivores,
meaning they only eat plants.

They love to graze on grass, but they've also been known to eat seaweed!

They have a special way of chewing that helps them digest food better.

Highland cows have four stomachs! Like all cows, they chew their food, swallow it, then bring it back up to chew again. This helps them break down tough plants and get all the nutrients they need.

Highland cows can weigh up to 1,300 pounds, and Highland bulls can weigh up to 1,800 pounds (about the size of a small car!).

Highland cows are very strong and can climb steep hills.

25
mph

They can run up to 25 miles per hour!

Highland cows are one of the oldest kinds of cattle in the world. They've been around since at least the 6th century.

They originated in the Scottish Highlands and the Outer Hebrides islands.

It's believed that during a visit to the Scottish Highlands, Queen Victoria showed great admiration for the distinctive red Highland cattle. Her fondness was said to have encouraged farmers to favor breeding the red variety, which helped it become more popular.

They are social animals and live in herds.

Highland cows have a dominance hierarchy, meaning older cows are in charge.

Highland cows have a special way of talking to each other. They use different sounds, like moos and grunts, to show how they feel or to call their calves. They also use body language such as moving their heads, tails, or ears, to show if they're happy, scared, or trying to warn others.

Highland cows are great moms! They take really good care of their calves and stay close to them. If there's danger, the mother cow will protect her baby and make sure it stays safe.

Highland cows might look tough with their big horns, but they are actually very gentle and calm.

Some Highland cows are so calm, they're used in therapy programs!

Highland cows are smart! They can recognize people and even remember them. If you're kind to a Highland cow, it might remember you the next time it sees you!

They are very independent and don't need much human help to survive.

Highland cows can live up to 20 years, much longer than most cattle.

Highland cows are popular in Scotland and are often seen in postcards and souvenirs.

Count the highland cows.

Thanks a bunch for diving into this!
Hope it brightened your brain with
some sparkling nuggets of wisdom!

If this book stole your heart,
don't be shy—shout it out
with a review!

BYE !

Check out these other interesting books in the Wonderful World of series!

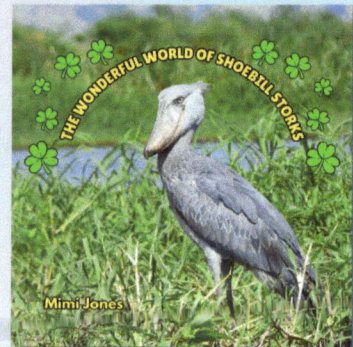

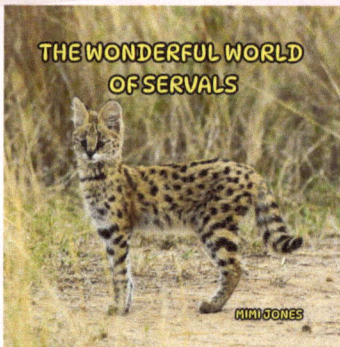

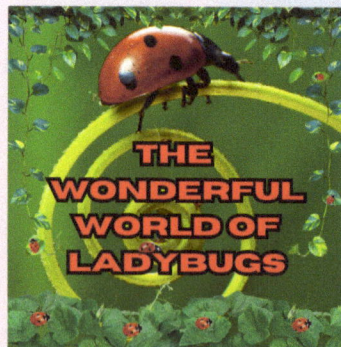

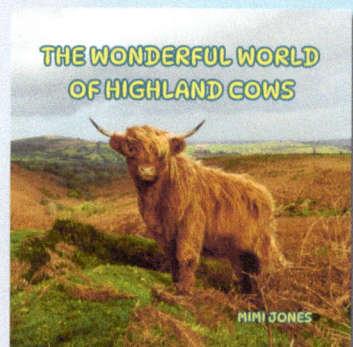

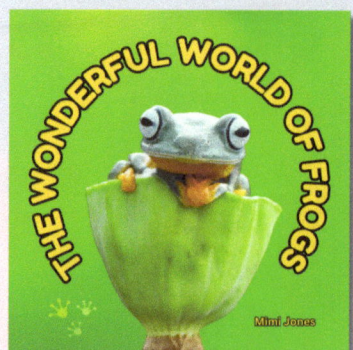

THE WONDERFUL WORLD OF SUNFLOWERS

THE WONDERFUL WORLD OF DRAGONFLIES
Mimi Jones

THE WONDERFUL WORLD OF SHOEBILL STORKS
Mimi Jones

THE WONDERFUL WORLD OF SERVALS
MIMI JONES

THE WONDERFUL WORLD OF LADYBUGS

THE WONDERFUL WORLD OF HIGHLAND COWS
MIMI JONES

THE WONDERFUL WORLD OF PANDAS
Mimi Jones

THE WONDERFUL WORLD OF RABBITS
Mimi Jones

THE WONDERFUL WORLD OF FROGS
Mimi Jones

www.mimibooks.com

www.ingramcontent.com/pod-product-compliance
Lightning Source LLC
Chambersburg PA
CBHW060835270326
41933CB00002B/95